*Suddenly, looking around,
they no longer saw anyone but
Jesus alone with them.
Mark 9:8*

**The intent and
purpose of this volume is to
give you faith, hope and
inspiration. Hopefully it will help bring
peace and tranquility into your life. May
it be a reminder of God's love, guidance
and His many blessings.**

**Our publications help to support our work
for needy children in over 120 countries
around the world. Through our
programs, thousands of children are
fed, clothed, educated, sheltered
and given the opportunity to
live decent lives.**

Salesian Missions wishes to extend special thanks and gratitude to ou[r] generous poet friends and to the publishers who have given us permission to reprin[t] material included in this book. Every effort has been made to give prope[r] acknowledgments. Any omissions or errors are deeply regretted, and the publisher, upo[n] notification, will be pleased to make the necessary corrections in subsequent editions.

Cover photo: © Punchstock/Design Pics

First Edition Printed in the U.S.A. by Concord Litho, Concord, NH 03301.

Moments of Solitude
from the
Salesian Collection

Compiled and Edited
by Jennifer Grimaldi

Illustrated by
Paul Scully, Bob Pantelone,
Russell Bushée, Terrie Meider,
Frank Massa, Dale Begley
and Robert VanSteinburg

Contents

Two Little Words

Two little words –
How important they are;
A message of peace
To light up the stars.
These two little words
Direct from the heart
Bring inner peace,
Ill feelings depart.
If we remember them always
As long as we live,
God's gifts will fill us
When we say, "I forgive."

Jacqui Richardson

I Can't Believe it's Springtime

I can't believe it's springtime,
But each blossom reveals it's so –
The hyacinth, the daffodil,
The green grass lushly grows.
Oh, hear the twitter of the birds
And feel the warmth return again.
Tiny hummingbirds will flit about
As springtime miracles descend.
Watch for the budding of the trees,
Smell the lilacs' fragrance in the air,
Touch the softness of a rose petal –
Ah, our God does truly care!
I can't believe it's springtime,
But the signs are everywhere –
From wee violets to hope renewed…
Spring's returned with all her flair.

Linda C. Grazulis

But I believe I shall enjoy the Lord's
goodness in the land of the living. Wait
for the Lord, take courage; be
stouthearted, wait for the Lord!
Psalm 27:13-14

And Not Believe in God

Who can see a springtime tree
That reaches forth majestically,
One tiny violet in the grass,
An April shower that hurries past,
A lovely blossom bursting wide,
The beauties of the countryside…
And not believe in God!

Who can see a clear blue sky,
A buzzing bee – a butterfly,
A Summer day when Junetime smiles,
A country road that travels miles,
That climbing hill that reaches high
To gently touch the far-off sky…
And not believe in God!

An Autumn tree with leaves of gold,
A Winter moment, brisk and cold,
An ever-soft December snow
That blankets all the world below,
The changing seasons – earth and sod…
And not believe there is a God.

Garnett Ann Schultz

Although you have not seen Him you love Him; even though you do not see Him now yet believe in Him, you rejoice with an indescribable and glorious joy.
1 Peter 1:8

Christ in Us

God's faithfulness is always there
To help a hurting friend...
A touch of kindness to a heart,
A joy that never ends.

Just when we feel all is lost,
His love comes pouring down...
Living water for the soul
And more to go around.

Every day we start anew,
This life we've come to know...
The best is truly yet to be;
His love will make it so.

Even sadness cannot dim
The light that lives inside...
Only Christ, the risen Lord,
Can keep us satisfied.

Jill Lemming

A Gift to Share

If I can write a poem a day
To cheer a soul along life's way,
Or lift someone from dark despair –
I'll know, dear Lord, Your words are there.

If I can make folks more aware
That for their neighbor they should care,
Can draw kind inward feelings out –
I'll be a friend beyond a doubt.

If I can show someone he's loved
Or point out blessings from above,
Can offer kind, consoling words –
I'll show the tenderness he deserves.

So grant me, Lord, this joyful gift
To guide and comfort those adrift,
And steer them safely to that shore
Where Your love shines forevermore.

Catherine Janssen Irwin

*If you come with us, we will
share with you the prosperity the
Lord will bestow on us.*
Numbers 10:32

Pilgrim's Journey

We wandered through a sea of grass,
My friend, the wind, and I,
And time stood still upon the hill
Beneath a cloudless sky.
We came upon a wooded glade
Which few had ever seen,
And stopped to rest among the best
Of pine and evergreen.

Barefoot we walked beside a brook
And heard a bluebird sing
A melody so sweet to me,
It was a sacred thing.
A hidden path led us astray,
My friend, the wind, and I,
Where flowers grew of every hue
So pleasing to the eye.

Sunflowers stood as tall as men,
But what hand placed them there
In a wooded glade within the shade
Where dreams fall light as air?
We wandered through a sea of grass
Upon our journey home,
And felt God there, as everywhere
Believers choose to roam.

Clay Harrison

For you had gone astray like sheep, but
you have now returned to the Shepherd
and Guardian of your souls.
1 Peter 2:25

May He grant you joy of heart and
may peace abide among you.
Sirach 50:23

Lasting Peace

There is no peace apart from God,
No matter where we go.
No scenes that will uplift for long
Or bring a lasting glow.

We need not search in places far
To find a sweet release
From all the little hurts and fears
That rob us of our peace.

The peace that passeth understanding
Is not of a man-made art,
For only God can fill the void
Within a restless heart.

If we but seek our Lord in prayer,
Trust in His will and way,
We'll find the peace within our hearts
We so yearn for today.

Kay Hoffman

..I will heal them, and reveal to them
an abundance of lasting peace.
Jeremiah 33:6

Grace, mercy, and peace will be
with us from God the Father and
from Jesus Christ the Father's
Son in truth and love.
2 John 1:3

God Is Here

I see God's softness in the clouds,
His beauty in the flowers,
His tenderness in motherhood,
His timelessness in hours.

I feel His power in a storm,
His warmth in the sunlight,
His gentle touch in a soft breeze,
His calming peace at night.

I feel His blessings with each hug,
His greatness in the sea,
I feel His grace in every smile,
I feel His love in me.

In everything I see and do
I feel His love and care.
I feel His kindness and His strength,
For God is always there.

Alice Higgins

*God is our refuge and our
strength, an ever-present
help in distress.*
Psalm 46:2

The Creator's Gift

The gentle blowing breeze
Nudges the lovely flowers
Into a dance, releasing
Rain from recent showers.

In the clear waters of a pond,
Goldfish play hide-and-seek,
Darting in, out, and around;
Beneath the water-lillies peak.

The melodious song of birds
Is heard as they build a nest
Where a newborn baby bird
Becomes the latest guest.

The distant purple mountains
To the heavens try to reach.
Far below, the rolling surf
Tosses waves upon the beach.

In this wonderful world
Are special gifts from the Creator's hand.
We thank and praise Him now
For everything so wonderful and grand.

Bernice Laux

Cast your care upon the Lord, who will give you support. God will never allow the righteous to stumble.
Psalm 55:23

God Cares for You

God watches all the birds that fly,
And places stars up in the sky.
He colors flowers and makes the rain
That glistens on the windowpane.

He's chosen each and every soul
That you will meet and love and hold.
He's picked the very best for you –
A family who will love you too.

If you should stumble along the way,
Just trust in God and always pray.
He cares for you and loves you so…
You'll never be alone, you know.

Clara Ashmore

*Cast all your worries upon Him
because He cares for you.*
1 Peter 5:7

Careful Spender

This day is a bright, new coin
  God granted me to spend.
Shall I buy treats and trinkets
  Or give to a needy friend?

Lord, I shall pray for guidance
With these few golden hours,
Seek many endless blessings,
  Sow faith's undying flowers.

When I was young and foolish,
  I lived beyond my means.
Each shiny coin was burning
  A hole inside my jeans.

Lord, now I've learned my lesson;
These rare days go so fast!
I count them like a miser,
For each may be the last.

Give coins before they tarnish
Or garments lose a seam…
I'll try to spend each moment
To mend a broken dream.

Maurice V. Bochicchio

I Yield Myself

What wonders do I see
As I travel down life's road?
They truly do amaze me
As I struggle with life's load.

God reaches out and lifts me
Out of the trials of life.
He's constantly walking with me,
Erasing fear and strife.

My life is ever in His hand
As He leads me every day.
I yield my all to Him
And throughout my life – obey.

Dona M. Maroney

What a Difference a Day Makes

What a difference a day makes
When you're trusting in the Lord,
Just to trust in His word
Will bring such a sweet reward.

Though downhearted and worried,
If we pray and believe
And give Him our burden,
Every care He'll relieve.

Though today may be testing,
Filled with trials and strife,
Tomorrow brings joy again
With His touch on your life.

Helen Gleason

Rejoice and leap for joy
on that day! Behold,
your reward will be
great in Heaven…
Luke 6:23

My Comforter

Has there ever been a time, my Lord,
When I cried out to You
That You didn't always answer me
And willingly help me through…

The problems that seemed unsolvable,
The pain that would not cease.
Then You held me close to You
And I felt Your sweet release.

No matter how hard or difficult
These burdens of mine might be,
I know that You are always there
To love and comfort me.

I might not see You physically,
But, oh, how I feel You near.
I sense Your presence close to me
And my burdens disappear.

You made a promise to me
That You would never depart
And would always remain with me
Within the confine of my heart.

Shirley Hile Powell

Autumn Glory

When leaves once budded in the Spring
Turn to burnished gold
Or scarlet red or russet brown
In splendor to behold…

It's then the world becomes for us
A magic place to stroll
Down winding, little country lanes
That stir our very soul.

Could Autumn be a hint of Heaven
With streets of shining gold
And colors even fairer still
Than ours so bright and bold?

Perhaps God gives us Autumn days
To lift our thoughts to Him.
He has the best in store for us.
By contrast, Fall is dim.

Margaret Peterson

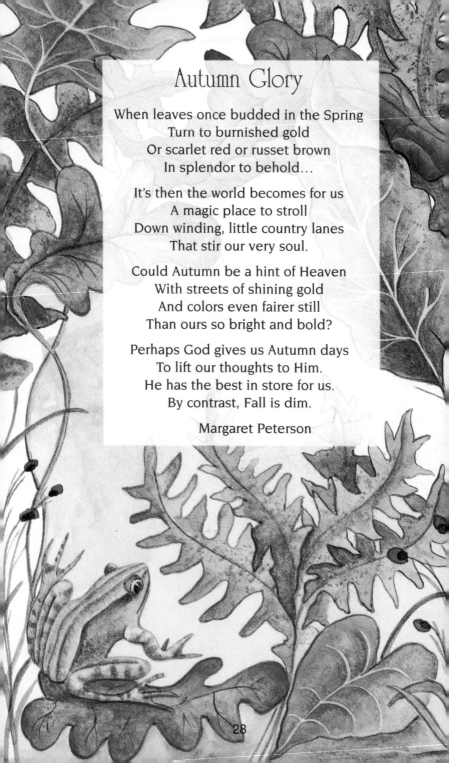

Seek His Kingdom

Seek ye first His Kingdom;
All else you've planned can wait…
God pleads for you to come to Him;
He's opened wide the gate.

The path you walk may be narrow,
But He'll make a way for you.
Just reach out for His outstretched hand
And He will lead you through.

All your problems He will solve,
On Him you can depend.
Because His heart's so full of love
And He's your dearest friend.

So, seek ye first His kingdom;
The best place to start
Lies within your being,
Deep down in your heart.

Lou Ella Cullipher

*But seek first the kingdom of God
and His righteousness, and all these
things will be given you besides.*
Matthew 6:33

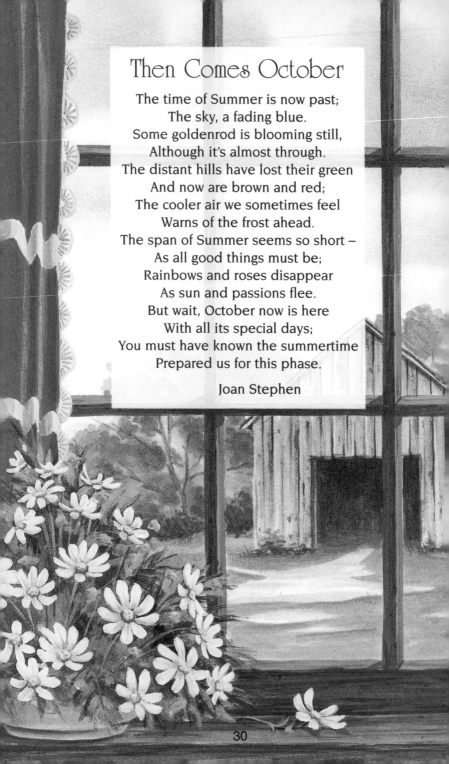

Then Comes October

The time of Summer is now past;
The sky, a fading blue.
Some goldenrod is blooming still,
Although it's almost through.
The distant hills have lost their green
And now are brown and red;
The cooler air we sometimes feel
Warns of the frost ahead.
The span of Summer seems so short –
As all good things must be;
Rainbows and roses disappear
As sun and passions flee.
But wait, October now is here
With all its special days;
You must have known the summertime
Prepared us for this phase.

Joan Stephen

Fading

How quickly do the colors fade
From the blossom of the rose,
How edges curl and crust to brown
And the stem no longer grows.
When life has waned and seasons end
And petals start to fall,
It's not the dying of the rose,
But its beauty we recall.

How would life be if love was like
The season of the flower?
How we would cherish every day,
Be blessed by every hour.
How differently we all would feel
That when the day passed on,
We remembered all the beauty
And not that it was gone.

Nancy Watson Dodrill

*I will remember the deeds of
the Lord; yes, Your wonders
of old I will remember.*
Psalm 77:12

Keep God in Your Life

When your faith wears thin,
And at times it will,
When the road you travel
Seems all uphill…
When you need more strength
To perform a task,
And could use more courage,
But you hate to ask…

Remember that God is waiting
Beside you night and day
To protect you and to help you
Through whatever comes your way.
He'll restore your faith
And give you strength for each task,
And all the courage you'll need,
If only you will ask.
Keep God in your life –
Whatever you may do,
And He will never turn
His eyes away from you!

Doris A. Orth

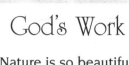

God's Work

Nature is so beautiful,
The flowers all around.
A walk in golden sunshine
Brings the great peace I've found.

The blossoms of red tulips
Kiss the clear, blue sky.
The clouds so white and fluffy
Touch the mountain peaks so high.

As the sun sets in the evening,
I feel God's presence upon the land.
The miracle of all dear life
Is embraced in God's own hand!

Alicia Slam

Simple Things

I marvel at the simple things
That leave my soul in wonder,
Like raindrops falling from the sky,
Streaking lightning and clashing thunder.

Majestic mountains capped with snow
Against an endless blue,
Flowers dancing on the wind
In meadows fresh with morning's dew.

Moonlight on the water still,
Reflecting Heaven's light,
Stars twinkling out their silent song
Bring peace to my heart this night.

Simple things are precious gifts
From God the creator of all.
His Spirit moving through all things
Whispers, "Come and listen to My call."

Donna Aucoin

I will listen for the word of God;
surely the Lord will proclaim peace
to His people, to the faithful, to
those who trust in Him.
Psalm 85:9

Tomorrow Comes

Today shall be a glorious day –
There is so much in store for me;
I'll walk along a forest path,
And admire snow-laden trees.

I'll listen to the sounds that rise
From deep within the wood;
I'll rest my spirit for a time
And dwell on all that's good.

I'll heed the din of raucous jays
And note the feathered flight
Of an owl disturbed from his perch –
And oh, a lovely sight!

I'll watch a rabbit hop about
And view a hidden fawn,
Its eyes grow timid in its fear –
I could go on and on.

All these gifts He gives to me
Though there are many more.
Tomorrow comes – a wondrous day –
What shall He have in store?

Henry W. Gurley

The Best Things Are Free

We should say it more often,
"The best things in life are free."
Like sunshine, laughter and rainbows
Or watching God color a tree.
Snowfalls that unfurl like velvet,
Boys and girls singing in school –
These are the things we cherish,
Living by the Golden Rule.
The music we hear in silence,
The love and the smiles from our soul,
All of these things cost us nothing –
They're free and they make each life whole.

Joan Stephen

The Shadow of His Hand

Beneath God's outstretched hand we walk
Each moment of the day…
In brightest days with skies of blue
Or when the sky is gray.

At times our souls may wonder why
The trials are so great,
Why plans, deep laid, can fall apart,
Why help can come too late?

No matter what may come to be,
God's chart is not unplanned.
The shadows that we feel are caused
By His great outstretched hand.

Margaret Peterson

*With mighty hand and outstretched
arm, God's love endures forever.*
Psalm 136:12

There's Always Room for Kindness

There's always room for kindness
Inside of you and me,
For opening our hearts up to others
Helps to set us free.
When we do a kindly deed,
Goodness will prevail.
God will never let us down;
His love never fails.
There's always room for kindness,
Whether big or small.
It may be you'll plant a daisy
Or grow an oak so tall.
To love is the best example
That anyone can give;
It's worth so much to others
And makes life such a joy to live.
There's always room for kindness –
A smile, a friendly nod –
But each action shared with generosity
Touches the very heart of God.

Linda C. Grazulis

Lord, You are kind and forgiving,
most loving to all who call on You.
Psalm 86:5

Our Father Calls

It would be nice to never leave
The comfort of God's fold,
To never take the challenges
That daily life can hold,
To never risk an unkind word
Or the hurt someone might cause;
To never shine the spotlight on
Our human cares and flaws.
But our Father calls His children
To step out in the night,
To reach out to a blinded world,
To be a shining light,
To measure words with loving care,
To share what we can give –
That they might know the Savior died
So humankind might live.

Nancy Watson Dodrill

My Savior Is Enough

Oh, the sweet name of Jesus,
Gentle Savior, gives me hope.
He's my strength and security,
My friend to help me cope.

Life isn't always easy
And my path sometimes is rough,
But I have found real joy and peace,
For my Savior is enough.

When days are dark and burdened
And when fear wants to control,
I just whisper, "Jesus"
And He's there to uplift and console.

Friends may not be faithful,
Disappointments may threaten me,
But I just look to Jesus
And allow Him my strength to be!

Nancy Janiga

Renaissance

I thank You, Lord, for reaching down
Into this wayward heart,
And granting me, with all my faults,
Your gift – a bright new start.

I doubted You, my heart was stone;
You knocked, I wouldn't heed.
Among the crowd, I was all alone,
Existing without Your creed.

Then one dark night, oppressed with sin,
A plea to You I cast.
The stone door cracked, You entered in –
My Savior… peace at last!

You gave me hope where dwelt despair;
You held me when I stumbled.
You lifted from me worry, fear;
I knelt before You, humbled.

You touched my soul, so sad and worn,
Directed toward disaster,
And graced me with new life – reborn!
Praise Jesus, Lord and Master.

Peggy Valday

*The Lord is my strength and my shield, in whom
my heart trusted and found help. So my heart
rejoices; with my song I praise my God.*
Psalm 28:7

We Are not Alone

Sometimes we fall into despair
And lose our faith and hope.
Our problems seem to magnify
And we don't know how to cope.

We struggle with life's daily trials
And begin to complain and moan.
We think our earthly battles
Must be fought by us alone.

But friends, let us remember
That our Savior is at our side.
He will fight our battles with us
And be our earthly guide.

He will carry us through the rough times
And calm our doubts and fears.
He will draw us close to His heart
And wipe away our tears.

So as we live our life on earth
And walk this earthly sod,
Let's remember that we are not alone
And put our faith and trust in God.

Shirley Hile Powell

God's Loving Promises

Rejoice with all creation,
Your soul be not forlorn,
For just as God assured us,
The Savior Christ was born.
With steadfast love God holds us,
Though life be dark and torn;
With guiding light in darkness,
He guarantees the dawn.
Now take the promises of God
And weave a fragrant lei
To wrap around your life
For strength throughout each day.

Gael Phaneuf

Worship

Lord, sitting in Your presence,
My heart can hear You speak.
In the stillness of dawn's breaking,
You bring my thirsty soul relief.

I meditate on Your kindness,
On who and what You are.
I read Your word of wisdom
And know You are not far.

My heart is filled with worship
And my lips are full of praise.
To You I give my glory;
To You my arms are raised.

Holy, holy, holy, Lord,
I lift high Your precious name.
I'm filled with Your Spirit
And I'll never be the same.

Nancy Janiga

Worship the Lord with cries
of gladness; come before
Him with joyful song.
Psalm 100:2

Throughout the Day

When the early dawn bids adieu
To the gently fading night
And the flowers lift their faces
To softly kiss the light…
Tis then, within your chamber 'lone,
Your heart should plant such seeds
That through the day will manifest
As good and loving deeds.
Then, as the fleeting hours pass
And the turmoil of the day
Envelopes 'round you like a cloud
To block your chosen way…
Tis then, within your inner heart,
This question should arise:
"Am I trying, striving, living,
As I would before His eyes?"

When the day is done and ended
And the world is hushed in sleep,
And over all the moon and stars
Their silent vigil keep…
Tis then that you should be prepared
To pass the Spirit's test –
Ah, what sweet joy to rest in Him
Knowing you've done your best!

Esther Nilsson

Don't Give Up

Don't give up – however things may seem;
Remember "it is darkest 'fore the dawn."
Hold up your head and straighten up your back;
Remember that you have to carry on!
Don't give up – that is the easy way;
Give life everything that you can give.
Don't be satisfied to drift along;
Learn how to cope – and how to really live!
Don't give up – there's more to you than that,
And you have faced much harder things before.
Cling to your courage and to your beliefs,
Trusting that whatever lies in store
Will always come about in such a way
That you can see the good Lord willed it so.
"You have to bear the cross to wear the crown"
Because this is the only way to go!

Grace E. Easley

Let us not grow tired of doing good,
for in due time we shall reap our
harvest, if we do not give up.
Galatians 6:9

Day by Day

Teach me, Lord, I humbly pray,
To live my life day by day,
Worrying not what tomorrow brings,
But always thankful for simple things.

The gift of life is Yours to give,
And we are judged by how we live.
Remind us, Lord, that while we're here
We have so very little to fear.

For You are in complete control,
And life is ours to have and hold
Until we finish our earthly deeds…
And then in Heaven You meet our needs.

Grant me the courage, the strength, the grace
To face the things that I must face,
Knowing full well that day by day,
You are with me in every way.

Marilyn Hinson

*I trust in Your faithfulness. Grant my heart
joy in Your help, That I may sing of the
Lord, "How good our God has been to me!"*
Psalm 13:6

More precious than gold is health and well-being, contentment of spirit than coral. No treasure greater than a healthy body; no happiness, than a joyful heart!
Sirach 30:15-16

Only Believe

When the road of life is rocky
And the toil too hard to bear,
Turn to Jesus Christ, our Savior –
You'll find the answer there.
Find the strength and find the knowledge,
Find the helping hand to take.
Only then you'll know contentment,
Living for your Master's sake.
The hand you hold will guide you,
Take you to the peaceful shore,
Where the waves of love engulf you,
Knowing God is with you evermore.

Edna Louise Gilbert

For wisdom will enter your heart,
knowledge will please your soul,
Proverbs 2:10

Country Road

I wonder where that old road goes –
The one they never paved.
It quietly climbs a distant hill
With memories it has saved…

The children who once ran with fun,
A farmer going to town,
The horses kicking up the dust
Before the rains came down.

The city at some distant end,
The trees that lined each side,
The Winter snows that drifted deep
Where only sleighs could ride.

The old road wanders on and on –
A narrow, roaming trail
Rising upward toward the sun,
Then dropping to some dale.

I hope they never pave that road –
Why spoil a peaceful past?
Somehow a rustic country road
Is something that should last.

Joan Stephen

*They found abundant and good
pastures, and the land was
spacious, quiet, and peaceful.*
1 Chronicles 4:40

Bless my Earnest Efforts

Lord, bless my earnest efforts,
I humbly beg of Thee;
Let me spread Your message,
Your servant let me be.
I seek no earthly glory
Nor vie for world acclaim...
Doing only now and always
My best in Jesus' name.
Fill my head with wisdom,
Add strength and guide my hand
That I may proclaim forever
The love You have for man.

Ranza Devereaux

When You're Alone

The days grow long when you're alone
And sometimes you feel blue;
You miss those who shared your life
And gave their love to you.

But memories will stay alive
And keep you company,
If you recall those precious years
Of loving harmony.

Remember, too, that God is near
And always there with you.
His presence and your faith in Him
Will chase away the blues.

Dolores Karides

*May the God of endurance and
encouragement grant you to think in
harmony with one another, in
keeping with Christ Jesus.*
Romans 15:5

God's Presence

I hear the voice of God proclaim
From loftiest of trees.
I can hear Him softly whisper
In the passing of a breeze.

I hear Him gently singing in
The rippling of a stream
And feel the warmth of His presence
In the dancing of a beam.

The sun upon the water
As it glides across with ease
Upon a sparkling lake
Or blue water of the seas.

I can sense His power in the thunder
And the lightning, oh, so bright.
I hear the ringing of His voice
In the twinkling stars at night.

Yet we need not travel up a mountain
Nor to the far-off seas –
We can sense His awesome presence
In prayer on bended knees.

Geraldine Borger

The birds of the air, the fish of the sea, and whatever swims the paths of the seas. O Lord, our Lord, how awesome is Your name through all the earth!
Psalm 8:9-10

Trusting the Lord

In valleys, on mountains, in sunshine or rain,
Trust in your Savior – you trust not in vain.
Great is His mercy, unfailing His love;
He sends sweet peace and joy from above.
He opens the heavens and blessings will flow
Upon His dear children that journey below.
So be of good cheer in sunshine or rain;
He is your Lord and He'll surely sustain
Your every need if only you ask.
He gives enough strength to complete every task.
Don't trust in riches which you may find,
For someday we all must leave them behind.
You will know peace and contentment each day
When you trust the Lord to show you the way.

Regina Wiencek

Renewal

If you are worried
And things go wrong,
If days seem endless
And nights are long…
Turn to the Lord.
In time of trouble,
In time of pain,
When storm clouds threaten
And you hope in vain…
He's there to help.
Your God will listen
If you but ask.
He will help you through
Your hardest task…
And show the way.
If you believe in
The power of prayer,
And put your life
Into His care…
He'll share your burden.
God's love for all
Will reach your heart.
His strength and courage
Will be the start…
Of your new life!

Helen M. Motti

*A clean heart create for me,
God; renew in me a
steadfast spirit.*
Psalm 51:12

63

The Lord replied, "If you have faith the size of a mustard seed, you would say to this mulberry tree, 'Be uprooted and planted in the sea,' and it would obey you."

Luke 17:6

Faith

A farmer lives by faith that's true,
Seeds once sown are out of view.
By faith he knows the seeds will sprout,
With faith and toil the grain heads out.
The joy of the harvest will then arrive,
And with that harvest faith will thrive.
A Christian lives by that faith too.
Words are seeds of faith sown by you.
God's Word once planted will surely sprout,
With love and prayer belief bursts out.
The joy of the harvest resides in God,
As faithful followers, you prepare the sod.
Keep that faith within your heart.
By words and actions that faith imparts.
Tell of the peace God's Word gave you
These faithful words will always hold true
The joy of the harvest comes from above,
So spread His Word with faith and love.

John Bammerlin

God indeed is my Savior; I am confident and unafraid. My strength and my courage is the Lord, and He has been my Savior.
Isaiah 12:2

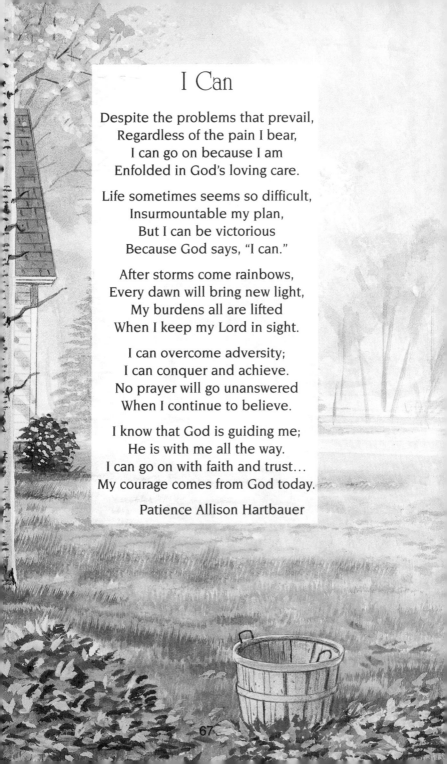

I Can

Despite the problems that prevail,
Regardless of the pain I bear,
I can go on because I am
Enfolded in God's loving care.

Life sometimes seems so difficult,
Insurmountable my plan,
But I can be victorious
Because God says, "I can."

After storms come rainbows,
Every dawn will bring new light,
My burdens all are lifted
When I keep my Lord in sight.

I can overcome adversity;
I can conquer and achieve.
No prayer will go unanswered
When I continue to believe.

I know that God is guiding me;
He is with me all the way.
I can go on with faith and trust…
My courage comes from God today.

Patience Allison Hartbauer

Trust

Put yourself in God's hands;
Trust Him every day.
He will always guide you,
Making clear the way.
You will cease to carry
The weight of fear and doubt
And always be contented
If you never leave God out.

Rachel Hartnett

November

The harvest yield is gathered in,
The air is crisp and clear,
Bright Autumn leaves have tumbled down,
For it's that time of year.

Songbirds have left their nests behind,
The garden's bedded down,
The butterfly and honeybee
Are nowhere to be found.

The gobbler struts in farmyard near,
The pumpkin's on the sill,
A hunter in his bright red vest
Heads for a nearby hill.

Though November skies are gray,
Hold fast this note of cheer,
For it won't be long until
Thanksgiving Day is here.

Kay Hoffman

*At dawn let me hear of
Your kindness, for in
You I trust. Show me the
path I should walk, for to
You I entrust my life.*
Psalm 143:8

The Plans of My Savior

The plans of my Savior
I cannot yet see,
Yet I know He has planned
What is best for me.

I don't need to see
'Round the bend in the road,
I only need help
With my daily load.

So trusting and living
One day at a time
Will bring gentle peace
To this heart of mine.

And when comes the time
He opens the door
That I might step through,
And be here no more...

'Tis then that I'll sing
And rejoice in His plan,
And be glad that I trusted...
And gave Him my hand.

Denise A. DeWald

Open My Eyes

Open my eyes that I might see
Thy blessed word at work in me,
Thy living truth that sets me free,
Blest words of life and liberty.

My falt'ring steps, Lord, guide today,
That from Thy truth I shall not stray;
Help me be strong in ev'ry way,
Thy holy Word to love, obey.

Open my heart to love Thee more,
Thy wondrous Son to serve, adore,
And when I reach Thy golden shore,
Thy praises sing forevermore.

Kathryn Thorne Bowsher

*With your own eyes you have
seen all these great deeds that
the Lord has done.*
Deuteronomy 11:7

Yellow Woods

Through October's glowing yellow woods,
I take my morning stroll.
I hear the melodies of Nature
While God speaks to my soul.

I hear the whisper of the playful wind
And feel its breath upon my face.
I marvel at the consummate beauty
Of this quiet and peaceful place.

The raucous caw of a distant crow
Sounds an ever-vigilant alarm.
His raspy off-key strident song
Adds harmony with resplendent charm.

I am as one with God and Nature,
Tho alone midst the yellow wood,
I pause to count my blessings –
And know that God is good!

Charles Clevenger

*Now then, stand ready to witness
the great marvel the Lord is about
to accomplish before your eyes.*
1 Samuel 12:16

Welcome to Our Nest

A house is never quite a home,
But just a place to rest,
Until we fill it up with love…
Then it becomes our nest.
Special friends who enter in
Bring with them special gifts.
They fill our hearts with memories,
Our lives, with happiness.
We know we'll never be alone
With God and friends so true,
For in our cozy, little nest
Each day brings something new.
Dreaming dreams that soon unfold,
Adventures taking flight;
Sharing all that God has done
And will do in each life.
We build our nests upon the Rock,
Then miracles come true.
As God has blessed us with our home,
He's blessed us twice with you.

Jill Lemming

*Welcome one another,
then, as Christ welcomed
you, for the glory of God.*
Romans 15:7

Tool

Each of us is like a tool
Waiting to be used,
Full of great potential that
Should never be abused!

The tool is never greater than
The hand that holds it fast.
No plan we have could equal God's,
Nor would our glory last.

But if we live not questioning,
Each day becomes a chance
To trust the master craftsman, God,
And thereby to advance…

To levels that are now unseen,
That rise to Heaven's land,
And all because we stayed within
The power of God's hand.

Margaret Peterson

The heavens declare the
glory of God; the sky
proclaims its builder's craft.
Psalm 19:2

Reaching the Lord

It isn't hard to reach the Lord –
He's with us night and day.
Kneel before Him earnestly;
Pour forth your heart and pray.
If you feel the need to cry,
He'll wipe your tear-stained face.
Reach out to Him, the Master waits,
And receive His love and grace.

Helen Parker

Road of Life

The road of life – a rough one
Where stumbling blocks abound,
But we'll make it to Heaven
When God our steps surround.

We'll keep our eyes upon Him,
Though the walk unsteady be,
For if we look unto the Lord,
Our steps He'll oversee.

And we'll surely rise above
The stumbling blocks all 'round
And walk with calm assurance
On safe and solid ground.

Josephine Anne Miller

*Those whose steps are guided by the
Lord; whose way God approves,
may stumble, but they will never
fall, for the Lord holds their hand.*
Psalm 37:23,24

The Daily Circle

For every flower sowed with love
Or cutting from a rose,
You'll see the labor's worth it when
A bit of beauty grows.

For every smile you cheerfully give
And gentle words you say,
You'll find returned a hundredfold
To brighten up your day.

For every time you pause to take
A child upon your knee,
That little time expands into
A lifetime memory.

For everyone you can forgive
Some hurt that's caused you grief,
Remember pain heals faster when
Your anger has been brief.

For every gift you gladly take
In payment just a smile;
The warmth that fills your heart with love
Has made the gift worthwhile.

For every struggle there's a gain
And effort is the cost,
But if we learn we can go on,
The lesson wasn't lost.

Accept the daily test of life
With love and hope and giving,
For truly through our joy or pain
We find the worth of living.

Billie Joan Wild

*It is the Lord's blessing
that brings wealth, and no
effort can substitute for it.*
Proverbs 10:22

God Is Always There

In our present world of sorrow,
Of heartache and despair,
Never feel alone, forsaken,
For God is always there.
When life's path is rough and rocky,
Seems more than we can bear,
There's a blessed Friend to guide you,
For God is always there.
We can overcome life's trials
And our many troubles bear,
For we have a faithful Helper –
Our God is always there.

Mary Eleanor Pitney

But I Can Trust My Lord

I may not know just how to believe
In miracles great and rare,
But I can put my trust in the Lord,
And know that He is there.

Each day is a triumph with my Lord,
As I read the Word and pray;
Somehow His grace and strength and love
Upholds me all the way.

O, how I love to trust my Lord
Through trials great and strong,
And prove how my Savior time again
Strengthens me with a song.

For better or worse, I'll trust You, Lord,
And find at the end of the day
How my wonderful Lord has carried me through
In a truly remarkable way!

Helen Neimy

Trust in the Lord with all your heart, on your own intelligence rely not; in all your ways be mindful of Him, and He will make straight your paths.
Proverbs 3:5,6

Influence

I stood beside the water's edge
And tossed a pebble small.
The ripples reached from shore to shore...
I watched them rise and fall.

The little things we do and say
Are like that tiny rock.
Some will bless and help to heal,
While others hurt and shock.

Influence reaches far and wide,
Like pebbles in the sea.
So this should be our daily prayer...
"Help me be more like Thee."

Anna M. Matthews

Patience

It takes a little time and faith
To ease the pain we bear –
It takes a little smile from friends
To let us know they care.
It takes a little hope and dreams
To help us bear the load
When we are trudging, so it seems,
Down a long and endless road.
It takes a lot of courage
To face the fiery darts
Of temptation and of sin
When they're aimed right at our hearts.
But we must be patient, wait a while…
Face the future with a smile,
For God above with His infinite love
Is never far away,
And it only takes a little prayer
To brighten up our day.

Lou Ella Cullipher

*With my whole being I
sing endless praise to You.
O Lord, my God, forever
will I give You thanks.*
Psalm 30:13

Touch Someone's Life

You can touch someone's life
With just a little smile.
An outstretched hand, a heartfelt hug,
Will help them through some trials…
Some words of wisdom and encouragement
To get them through the day,
The love of Jesus seen through you
Will help them find their way!
So when you see a saddened face,
Reach out and touch their heart.
Take the time to show them love –
A smile's the way to start!

Millie Torzilli

God Is Beauty

Have you seen a sunrise
That sets the world aglow?
Then you've seen the God I love,
You've seen the God I know.

Have you seen a sunset
That puts the world to rest?
Then you've seen my dearest Friend,
The one that I love best.

Have you seen a starlit night
In all its majesty?
Then you've seen the very One
Who means the world to me.

Have you seen a lovely rose
Whose fragrance fills the air?
Then you've seen my Shepherd
And His beauty everywhere.

Have you seen a baby smile
Or watched a teardrop fall?
If you have, you've seen my King
My Lord, who's Lord of all.

Betty Purser Patten

*Splendor and majesty go before Him;
praise and joy are in His holy place.*
1 Chronicles 16:27

His Presence

A friend of mine once asked me
Just how could I believe
In someone whom I never saw,
Nor spoken words receive.

I thought, perhaps I should explain
Just why I have no doubt
That it was God's creativeness
That brought this world about.

I only have to look around
To know that He is there.
I see, and feel, and hear Him –
That's why I'm so aware.

I see Him in the raindrops
That nourish trees and flowers.
I see Him in the rainbows
That sometimes follow showers.

I hear Him when a meadowlark
Trills out its joyful song.
I hear Him when the thunder
Comes forth so loud and strong.

For those who wish to listen,
It is played throughout the land,
The symphony of life itself
Directed by His hand.

Alora M. Knight

His World

I walked within God's world today,
Across wide open ground,
And felt soft breezes brush my face
While listening to each sound.

A sunken swampland lay transformed
In beds of lavender flowers,
And a hummingbird sipped sweet nectar
As he flitted through this bower.

Bright songbirds sang their music
When I crossed a wide open field,
And found white blackberry blossoms –
They promised a bounteous yield!

While savoring all this beauty,
I retraced my steps toward home;
Thanking and praising God above
With a heart on overflow.

Lola Neff Merritt

Nature's Quilt

Mother Nature spread a quilt
Upon the vistas wide,
Made of daisy patches bright –
'Twas with pink clover tied.

Hemmed with purple asters,
The wild and vivid kind,
With black-eyed Susan corners
And tufts of milkweed lined.

This quilt of lovely colors,
In free-form grand array,
Like a precious work of art
Upon the land did lay.

Virginia Borman Grimmer

*Adorn yourself with
grandeur and majesty,
and array yourself with
glory and splendor.*
Job 40:10

What Is Love?

Love is a wonderful feeling
Felt deep within the heart.
It's knowing and it's caring –
It's God's precious work of art.

Love makes the Winter turn to Spring
And dark clouds go away.
It gives a burst of energy
To each and every day.

It takes much care and nourishing,
Just as a tiny flower,
And yet it grows beyond all boundaries
With its wondrous power.

Love is God's special medicine
To make the whole world new.
A treasure and a blessing
For all of us, it's true.

It feeds the heart, cleanses the soul,
Gives strength to every day.
It makes our lives so pure and new
In its own special way.

Like a circle, love goes around
And it is very true,
If you give love out freely,
It will soon return to you.

God blessed us with this treasure
We must care for tenderly,
And then we'll know what God's love means
And what it's meant to be.

Edna Louise Gilbert

t there too you shall seek the Lord, your God; and
you shall indeed find Him when you search after
Him with your whole heart and your whole soul.
Deuteronomy 4:29

If I Could Borrow

If I could borrow a bonnet
From the golden daffodil
And fragrance from the roses
That bloom on my windowsill…

Take diamonds from the dew drops
And the rainbow's pot of gold;
If the peace of the forest
Was mine to have and hold…

If the notes of the songbirds
Were mine to sing each day…
Would not my life be richer
Than before they came my way?

Dottlee Duggan Reid

The Earth Is Filled
With His Tender Love

The earth is filled with His tender love;
It reaches from ocean to ocean,
And angels descending from Heaven above
Sing of our Savior's devotion.

The birdsongs at dawning and all through the day
Sing of His love in their own special way,
And flowers that bloom in the Spring of the year
Seem to be whispering, "Jesus is near."

The earth is filled with His tender love;
With blessings, the world He's bestowing,
For sinners rejecting His wonderful love,
Jesus' love keeps on growing.

Growing like flowers with warm April rain,
Pure as the sunlight that floods golden grain;
The sun, moon and stars in their places above
Shine down His glorious, infinite love.

Lou Ella Cullipher

*Shout joyfully to God, all you
on earth; sing of His glorious
name; give Him glorious praise.*
Psalm 66:2

95

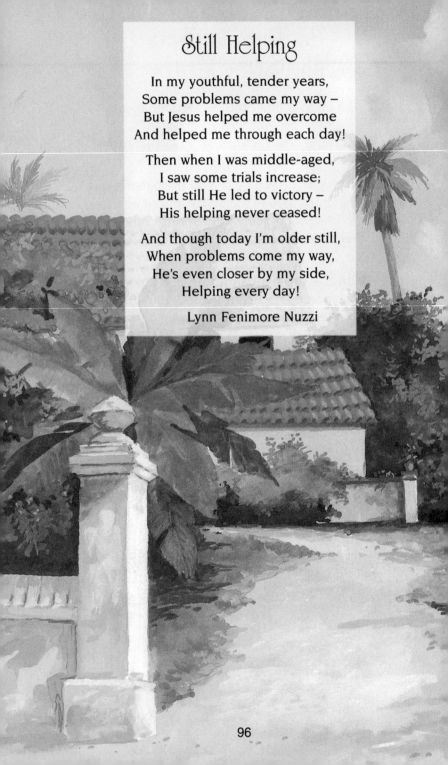

Still Helping

In my youthful, tender years,
Some problems came my way –
But Jesus helped me overcome
And helped me through each day!

Then when I was middle-aged,
I saw some trials increase;
But still He led to victory –
His helping never ceased!

And though today I'm older still,
When problems come my way,
He's even closer by my side,
Helping every day!

Lynn Fenimore Nuzzi

Talents

It would be such a dull world
If we were all the same.
Our Lord provides some talents
That each of us may claim.

Some people can write poems,
And some can truly sing.
Some know how to build a house
And fix 'most anything.

Some paint such lovely pictures,
And some of us can teach.
Some can plow a field of corn,
And some are called to preach.

If we were all the same,
We'd find it dull each day.
Thank God for different talents…
He planned it all that way!

Edna Massimilla

*There are different
kinds of spiritual gifts
but the same Spirit.*
1 Corinthians 12:4

Love

Love is such a wondrous thing –
There's nothing it can't do.
Love can take a troubled life
And make it bright and new.
It can change your outlook
From dark and deep despair,
To one of hope and confidence
Because somebody cares.
Love is such a happy thing –
It makes you feel alive.
When someone says, "I care for you,"
You're filled with joy inside.
It really lifts your spirits
To have a loving friend
Who's close to you, no matter what,
And will be to the end.

Love is such a blessing –
How empty life would be
If no one ever whispered,
"You mean a lot to me."
It takes a special person
To hurt when you are sad,
And maybe shed a tear with you
Or smile when you're glad.
Love is knowing Jesus –
He means so much to me.
He gladly gave up Heaven,
From sin to set me free.
I may not understand such love
Or why it had to be,
But I can gladly tell the world
What love has done for me.

Audrey Shoemaker

Tomorrow Is Another Day

Tomorrow is another day
To live and laugh and dream and play,
To watch a purple sunset sky,
To never, ever say good-bye.

Tomorrow is another chance
To hope and smile and sing and dance,
To wish upon a falling star,
To catch a firefly in a jar.

Tomorrow is another day
To care and give and help and pray,
To fill a hopeless heart with glee,
To live my life in dignity.

Nora M. Bozeman

*She is clothed with strength
and dignity, and she laughs
at the days to come.*
Proverbs 31:25

Peace

No matter where you travel
While in your quest for peace,
You'll find there's always something
To block the stress release.

Serenity of Nature,
In all its beauty rare,
Can help relieve the pressure
Brought on by daily care.

But here's a bit of wisdom
I share 'fore you begin…
Your time is wasted searching
'Til you have peace within.

An inner-peace is priceless…
It helps you through the day
To keep things in perspective
When troubles come your way.

Anna M. Matthews

*Relieve the troubles of
my heart; bring me
out of my distress.*
Psalm 25:17

A Little While

We're only here a little while –
Life is a fragile thing.
So short a time can be our own
For pauper or for king.
Life never offers guarantees
Of what tomorrow holds.
We do our best without complaint
As each new day unfolds.
A little while – one moment brief –
An hour – a day – a week,
The miracle of life and death
We all so fondly seek.

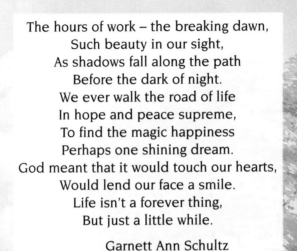

The hours of work – the breaking dawn,
Such beauty in our sight,
As shadows fall along the path
Before the dark of night.
We ever walk the road of life
In hope and peace supreme,
To find the magic happiness
Perhaps one shining dream.
God meant that it would touch our hearts,
Would lend our face a smile.
Life isn't a forever thing,
But just a little while.

Garnett Ann Schultz

Lean on Me

Are you walking a dreary road, My child,
And are burdened down with care?
Lean on Me, your burdens yield;
Your heavy load I'll bear.

Are you thinking that no one really cares
And you're walking all alone?
Lean on Me, your troubles share;
I'll make them all My own.

Are you weary of facing each new day
And are fearing what's ahead?
Lean on Me, the Truth, the Way;
I'll give you peace instead.

Kathryn Thorne Bowsher

*Come to Me, all you who
labor and are burdened,
and I will give you rest.*
Matthew 11:28

The Loving Hand of God

When life with all its struggles
Just seems to pass you by,
True happiness is gone from life,
You only sit and sigh…

The joy is gone from living,
The tears run down your face,
The world is full of sorrow
Which time cannot erase…

The only way to ease the pain
Is to take hold of God's hand.
It will uplift and guide you
Through the barren, lonely land.

God will plant your feet upon a rock,
Give you peace and courage, too,
And you will never feel alone…
He will always be with you.

Frances Culp Wolfe

*Yet I am always with
you; You take hold of
My right hand.*
Psalm 73:23

Let My Soul Keep on Praying

Life becomes perplexed at times
And sunshine dims its light;
It's then I call upon the Lord
For strength throughout the night…

And let my soul keep on praying.

I'll pray for all good things in life
So that I may share with others.
I'll love my neighbor as myself;
Desiring harmony with one another…

And let my soul keep on praying.

I'll conquer life's many trials
With my Savior at my side.
I'll strive to do His holy will
And in His love abide…

And let my soul keep on praying.

I'll pray with all of my heart
That peace will come to earth.
I'll pray to always honor God
And prove to Him my worth.

Let my soul keep on praying!

Shirley Hile Powell

My soul, be at rest in
God alone, from whom
comes my hope.
Psalm 62:6

God is our refuge and strength,
a very present help in trouble.
Psalm 46:1

Trials Are Only Shadows

Trials are only shadows
That fall upon our path;
Just like earthly shadows,
They never come to last.
They're but a mere hiatus
Amidst our span of life;
They last but just a moment
And then they take their flight.

Trials are merely shadows
That cross the lane of life;
They come to serve a purpose
And then they fade from sight.
If we'll just keep on trusting
Our Savior and our Guide,
He'll bring us through these shadows
Into His glorious light.

Loise Pinkerton Fritz

*Rise up in splendor! Your
light has come, the glory of
the Lord shines upon you.*
Isaiah 60:1

The Gifts

Looking one morning at God's beautiful sea
And the wondrous gifts He has given to me,
I knew it was time for my arms to upraise.
To God be the glory. To Him be the praise.

For so many blessings that I take for granted,
The sound of the crest of the wave when it landed,
The gift of my hearing the song from a bird,
The whispered "I love you" from God I just heard.

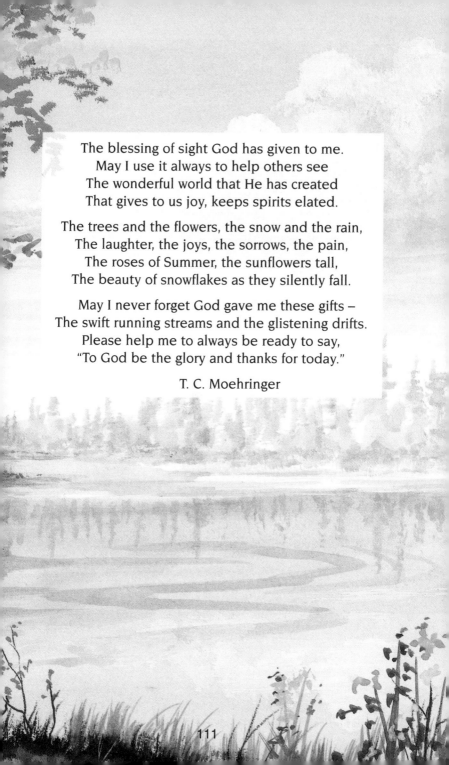

The blessing of sight God has given to me.
May I use it always to help others see
The wonderful world that He has created
That gives to us joy, keeps spirits elated.

The trees and the flowers, the snow and the rain,
The laughter, the joys, the sorrows, the pain,
The roses of Summer, the sunflowers tall,
The beauty of snowflakes as they silently fall.

May I never forget God gave me these gifts –
The swift running streams and the glistening drifts.
Please help me to always be ready to say,
"To God be the glory and thanks for today."

T. C. Moehringer

Through Bare Branches

I loved the leafy Summer trees,
But now there stretches wide
Beyond my window casement
A view bare limbs can't hide.
I clearly see the sunset,
I plainly see the stars,
Now there are no Summer leaves
The distant view to mar.
I mourned to see them falling.
What they hid I did not know,
The view they had been hiding
Until God bade them go.
Now looking up I see birds in flight
And wonder, could it be
That by losing other precious things
Extend life's view for me?

Minnie Boyd Popish

Summer Is Fading, Fading Away

Summer is fading, fading away,
Changing, unwinding every day.
The leaves are turning crimson and gold,
Getting brighter as each day unfolds.
Autumn's emerging from Nature's cocoon,
Spreading its wings by the light of the moon.
Each morning is precious, shiny and new,
As frost on the pumpkin replaces the dew.
Words can't describe, nor can they convey
The breathtaking beauty of all I survey.
Yes, Summer is fading like yesterday's rose,
But Autumn is wearing her finest new clothes.
The seasons keep changing, revolving each day;
Now Summer is fading, fading away,
But somewhere in the asters, the bright goldenrod,
My faith is renewed by the presence of God!

Clay Harrison

*A clean heart create
for me, God; renew in
me a steadfast spirit.*
Psalm 51:12

Come, Holy Spirit

I knock, Holy Spirit, here at Your door,
Needing Your grace but deserving no more.
The hour is late and Your lights are out,
Although I have hope, I wrestle with doubt.
Here in the dark, the night air is chilled…
Come, Holy Spirit, remember me still.

I wait, Holy Spirit, here by the shore,
Sensing Your goodness and mercy once more.
The wind whispers softly, surrounding my heart.
Although I have faith, I wait in the dark.
Here in my soul, expectation begins...
Come, Holy Spirit, come let me in.

I pray, Holy Spirit, here in the night,
Seeking Your presence and needing Your light.
Yet even today I whisper and call,
Yet even today I stumble and fall.
Here in the world, my body grows old...
Come, Holy Spirit, come make me whole.

I wait, Holy Spirit, here for Your time,
Doing my penance, preparing my mind.
The sins of the past dissolve through Your grace,
Behind the cracked door, Your mercy awaits.
Here at the threshold, I whisper Your name...
Come, Holy Spirit, come fill me again.

John Zurn

Trust in Him

When your heart is heavy
And the light of life grows dim,
Take your problems to Jesus
And put your trust in Him.
Give up your cares completely
And discipline your mind
To communicate with Jesus,
The Savior of mankind.

Dorothy Kohlberger

Our Heavenly Home

We praise You and we bless You, Lord,
For all the things You are.
You made us in Your image,
Yet we stray from You so far.

Your love has given us so many things,
And yet we turn away.
We ask You for the grace and help
To guide us on our way.

We thank You for our blessings
And for our sufferings, too,
For it's how we handle joys and woes
That will bring us home to You.

So guide us, Lord, and help us
That to Your will we hold.
Please lead us home to Heaven
To share Your crown of gold.

Georgiann Donovan

*Grace to you and peace from
God our Father and the
Lord Jesus Christ.*
1 Corinthians 1:3

Brotherly Love

You search our hearts
And know us, Lord.
Are we worthy
To reap Your rewards?

Prepared for the time
Not too far away
When You might ask us, Lord,
Did you visit Me each day?

Did you share your love with others,
Those you met along the way,
Perform a kind deed or two
To help brighten someone's day?

Did you clothe and shelter Me,
Lend a helping hand,
As I watched My people
Sharing the sorrows of their lands?

Did you daily walk with Me,
Seek the guidance of My light,
Being faithful within your heart,
Helping others in their plight?

Jacqui Richardson

God Is So Amazing

Our God is so amazing,
He meets our every need.
It may not be the way we think,
But He harvests all our seeds.

He's always there when things go wrong;
We don't have to walk alone.
Each time we feel downhearted,
He fills our hearts with song.

We never have to question
When things don't go our way,
'Cause He is there to be our Friend,
To guide us through each day.

Yes, our God is so amazing,
He knows what's best for all.
He's always there to be our Friend
And He answers when we call.

Bonnie J. Knapp

The Lord is my strength and my shield, in whom my heart trusted and found help. So my heart rejoices; with my song I praise my God.
Psalm 28:7

Turn to God

Turn to God for any need,
Follow Him and let Him lead.

Ask God for help when in sorrow,
All His comfort is yours to borrow.

Follow God and let Him lead,
His love for you fills every need.

Grasp God's hand and let Him guide,
Look up to Him – stay at His side.

Turn to God any time, any day,
He will help you find your way.

William Bredesen

Praise Song

The mountains rise in harmony
As they press against the sky.
The jet-blue lake, serene and still,
The forests sing nearby…

A deer runs wild in freedom's path;
He greets a new day's morn.
The snows send anthems in the air,
Our spirits are reborn.

Norma Woodbridge

Between Twilight and the Sunrise

Between twilight and the sunrise
When stars come out to play,
Prayers wing their way to Heaven
With each new breaking day.
Some pray for fame and fortune;
Some ask for daily bread,
While others simply praise Him
For shelter and their bed.
Some pray with teardrops flowing
For broken hearts to mend,
Still others ask for guidance
For family and friend.
Prayers wing their way to Heaven
With promises to keep
Between twilight and the sunrise
While the world is fast asleep.

Clay Harrison

*Shout with joy to the Lord,
all the earth; break into
song; sing praise.
Psalm 98:4*

Comfort Words

When words won't come to speak my heart
And empty space without prevails,
Lord, help whatever words I say;
Just calm life's stormy, mighty gales.

Your are the Beacon in the storm,
You are the Light along the way.
When I cry out, "What can I do?"
Please give me comfort words to say.

I look about and see such pain;
I hear the cries of those You love.
I see the teardrops on each face;
I kneel before Your throne above.

You said that there would never be
A load too heavy, Lord, to bear.
I need the words to somehow say,
"I hurt with you – I really care."

I do not understand at all
Just why this pain must somehow be,
And yet I want to know the way
To let Your comfort flow through me.

Gertrude B. McClain

A Crown of Smiles

When life sometimes brings heartache
And problems wear us down,
We still should not be worried,
And try not to wear a frown.
For life is sometimes trying
And disappoints us all,
But we can call on Jesus
Who lifts us when we fall.
We should all remember
That life can be worthwhile,
If we can keep from frowning
And wear a crown of smiles!

Sancie Earman King